SPAIN-

November, 2004

- The World & How To Get There -

♏ ♐

Robert J. Schulenburg

Spain - November, 2004
The World *&* How To Get There
by Robert J. Schulenburg
Copyright © 2012 Robert J. Schulenburg

Same Strange World Press
PO Box 43652
Tucson, AZ 85733-3652

Or Email us at:

info@samestrangeworld.com

Visit us on the web at:

www.samestrangeworld.com

Dedication –

*This log is Dedicated to Bryan Dwyer,
who knows what it is like to be in It
and said I should write about It.*

The World & How to Get There
By Way of Introduction

My name is Robert J. Schulenburg, Rob to my friends, and I am legally blind. I do not need a white cane to travel independently, and I can read print just fine. But, I do occasionally bump into people. I can't read the newspaper without touching my nose to the page. I do not look disabled and have never considered myself handicapped. This is my greatest advantage and my most beguiling curse.

In the 367 days that passed between February 13th, 2004 and February 14th, 2005, a full leap year plus a day, I traveled across the country and across the world. I saw the Southern Cross and the Midnight Sun. In between I fell in love, twice, broke up, once, and got married, by almost all accounts, on accident.

And there was so much more…

One man, one world, one year. This is one of those stories that happened in between.

Spain
November, 2004

Look for the absurd, and you will find it. Expect the absurd and it will find you. Respect the absurd, and you may survive it.

* * *

At quarter till ten we paid for breakfast and wandered subconsciously to the security checkpoint. The flight was at 10:40 with boarding beginning at ten after ten.

Happy goodbyes involving kisses and the insistence I find a girlfriend while I was away were interrupted by the persistence of people in lining up behind us, no matter how far to the side we'd move away from the people checking the boarding passes. When we arrived there was nobody entering the terminal. But, in the cultural tradition of lines everywhere, one was formed as soon as two or more were gathered in its name.

The line split as soon as I got in and I pulled the wrong half of the wishbone. While distinctly shorter, luck was not with me, as everyone between me and the domestic security professional had not seemed to understand the concept of a picture ID.

As I've observed, on a freeway, it is the exact same moment that you get stuck behind a truck that a line of highly intelligent motorists materializes behind you and begins modeling the concept of going around slow moving traffic. Unfortunately, the quick study is kept to the end of the lecture as car after car, truck after truck, and, inevitably, semi after semi, directly behind you keeps you trapped in the auditorium wishing you could start hurling spitwads at everyone else to pass the time.

Tourist traffic flowed mockingly around and past me as a grandmother was asked for a driver's license.

My boarding pass was checked and I was instructed to put my passport away, as if I had offended protocol. Shame on me for deviating from the script. With my ID out and ready to go my uniformed counterpart in this little drama was at a loss for words, the only words apparently at the ready being, "I'll need to see your picture ID." I entered one of several lines for security and began taking off my boots.

I had thought about this; what to wear. Usually cold and uncomfortable on an airplane before I go to sleep, I went with a long sleeve dress shirt and a pair of slacks. This meant I was wearing boots. My thinking was that if I have to spend nearly a full day in transit, I'm going to look like crap when I arrive. How much crap I looked like was up to me.

I've traveled to plenty of other places where being obviously worn by the road upon arrival could be an asset. But I hadn't been to Europe for a while, and I wanted to look nice.

Something in the back of my mind told me that sneakers, ripped jeans, and a flannel shirt may have been expedient and comfortable when traveling to

Alaska, or Tennessee. But flying through England, by comparison, was like the difference between going to a neighborhood block party and attending dinner at a rich second cousin's house who you know privately considers you to be trailer trash, but still not worthy of charity.

Boots were a necessary inconvenience, I had decided. I wanted to make a good impression. You know, so Europe would like me.

So, I began to disrobe in line. Boots, jacket, belt, emptied pocket-contents, they all went into their respective trays and bins and began their caravan through the x-ray machine.

I noticed that about four people in line ahead of me were behind me when I was showing off with my passport a minute earlier. I have no idea how they got ahead of me. Life Lesson: Just like in a kung fu movie, never take your eyes off your opponent while waiting in line for airport security, even when taking off your boots.

My bag went through twice.

It was now 10:15. I picked up my boots and carried them down to the gates to put them on when I got in line to board the flight.

Long rectangular dark signs began to slip by overhead as I made my way through the terminal. Gates 1-4, with an arrow. I passed a bar and a gift shop. Gates 5 through whatever, with another arrow. (I stopped paying attention to the numbers as my pace increased.) I needed 24. Further down the rabbit hole, I hit a dead end at Gate 14.

Wrong Terminal.

A security guard informed me that I had to leave the security area, turn right, and go down to the other end of the facility. He told me not to worry because, "It's not a very big airport."

At that time, at that place, that was not what I needed to hear. There is such a thing as, say, a Big Taco Bell and a Small Taco Bell. But I was not in a Taco Bell. I was in an International Airport. And while it only took me a few minutes to sprint past ticket counters and restaurants in my stocking feet, boots in hand, to the other end of the complex, this man's perspective on the relative grandeur involved when having to sprint anywhere was not appreciated.

What I was appreciating at the moment was that I had gone past two people checking my boarding pass into the wrong terminal, and that I was wearing comfortable, clean, socks. My mother would be so proud.

Ironies and Preparedness Paying Off. Variety may be the spice of life, but these are the whipped cream and sprinkles.

One old man, and a mother traveling with four children were all that stood between me and my flight when the minute hand came around to 10:25. As the mom explained to her charges that her youngsters could keep their coats on, keep their shoes on, take their backpacks off, and yes, the littlest could be carried through the security gates, I filled bins and trays with an efficiency that distracted and awed her children.

The old man, in the meantime, reluctantly took off his shoes and asked for his jacket back so he could get his boarding pass out. Once the belt on the machine was moving again, the mother and I began leading our bins and feeding our belongings through. We were immediately victimized by a series of geriatrics limping past us with an assortment of metal body parts but no carry-on items. (See previously cited Life Lesson). This is the airport equivalent of writing a check in the five items or less line, the similarity only emphasized by the offending parties not having any picture ID.

At 10:35 I was putting my boots on at the end of the jetway, daring the flight crew with a stare to close the door on me.

My eyes never left theirs as I did up my laces.

* * *

As the steward demonstrated how to use a seatbelt, I noticed that there was gum stuck to the arm of my seat. Someone had tried to pry or scrape it at one point, but it was there, on the end of the armrest, next to the wall and just where your fingers would curl under to.

This is what banning smoking on domestic flights has brought us to. Gum on the armrests instead of crammed into the ashtray where it belongs.

The seatbelt worked just as I had been told to expect it to. Seatbelts but no ashtrays. Because there was no smoking anymore. That's what they call progress. I wondered how long until the airlines installed airbags.

* * *

I went to the bathroom. Imagine my surprise to find an ashtray on the inside of the door to the lavatory. So much for progress. I checked. No gum. There was a very creative icon of a cigarette butt crumpling under the force of an invisible hand, complete with accordion folds by the smoking lit end.

This is why signs are important. They remind us that there are things you shouldn't do even though you can. This is how an airplane bathroom is like the Garden of Eden. Yes there's a tree whose fruit will impart the total knowledge of Good and Evil unto those who may eat of it. But don't eat that fruit. Yes, it's there. Just ignore it. God should have put up a sign with a clever icon. Perhaps one with human beings being crushed under an invisible hand, complete with accordion folds on the smoking lit end.

I looked around. I was surrounded by icons. There were three around the room on the walls, two on either side of the toilet seat, and one at sitting eye level on the wall opposite the sink. These indicated that one's hand should not deposit into the toilet feminine hygiene products, batteries, plastic water bottles, Dixie cups, and something that could only be described as a hanky- the way it was pinched and hung from forefingers and thumb.

To my right was an icon to indicate where hankies could be safely released. Under this sign, on the same swing door, was an icon indicating that that particularly specific receptacle was not an ashtray. The lock had a picture of a lock over it that was next to a sign above the ashtray indicating that smoking was prohibited. Above me, on a hinged shelf was an indication that the plastic sheet that was ready to fall on my head at the first sign of turbulence was a baby changing table. To my left, and behind me, was a dispenser of feminine hygiene products. This picture shared a door with vomit receptacles. Both logos were more abstract, implying the sense, rather than the form or specific shape, as you would imagine.

I began looking for words.

On the back of the door I found, "Lavatory Smoke Detector Installed". Directly below it; a sign indicating the federal fine for tampering with the detector. Below the locks, "Close door for take off and landing". I wondered who had to go in and do that. Directly above the toilet, "Please use the trash containers for anything other than toilet tissue." And below that, "Discarding anything other than toilet tissue in the toilet can cause external leaks and create a safety hazard". I've read this one before. It seems to be a standard. It always summons the most amazing images in my head.

I was awash in doctrine. Signs and portents surrounded me dictating what could and couldn't go where. Things I had never considered bringing into or disposing of in an airplane bathroom (batteries? Really?) all had there prescribed and specifically prohibited depositories.

And yet something was missing. Something critical to what I had assumed was the basic function of the toilet.

I was struck with bemused panic. Had I doomed us all? Had I been doing it wrong all these years? Where was I supposed to...? I prayed for a sign, but there was none.

* * *

The American Way Magazine in my seat pocket did not proclaim itself to be an award winning publication. I had traveled facing magazines that made this claim and wondered why any magazine wouldn't bother to be award winning. Or at least to proclaim itself to be. Who would know? What passenger in Coach would care?

Bon Jovi stared back at me from the front cover, daring comment. I studied the terminal maps and put the magazine back with the so-you're-about-to-die picture book and vomit receptacles.

* * *

Arriving in Dallas I was informed that the next flight to Gatwick would be departing from Terminal A. Deciding to make a play for it, I went down the escalators to catch the airport shuttle train to the next complex, and waited for the crowd to thin as train after train slowly emptied the station.

When I finally boarded the car was occupied but not crowded. We all found seats, mine near the back of the car. My neighbor peered critically to the front, then past me to the back. As the recording informed us of the dangers of standing near doors, he observed, "There ain't nobody driving this thing. There ain't no people. It's all computers." He seemed troubled and confused. Then added, "That just ain't right. They shouldn't be driving' folks around like that with just computers."

The train took off.

Despite his initial trepidation, my neighbor supplied a running commentary for the next four minutes of the technical wonders at play on our journey. As we descended and slowed around a turn, the rest of us in the car were informed, "Those are them magnetic curbs. They's there to keep the train on the rails and for to slw'n us down on the curves."

I was stunned.

Upon entering a terminal, the car at large was informed, "Those lights came on." He pointed up, "They wasn't on before, but they turned on when we went inside."

He was right.

As we pulled up to the next station, a recording told us we were approaching Terminal A. Sure enough, "That's another computer. It's telling us where we'll be getting off at."   As the doors opened, he seemed relieved and extremely pleased with himself at the same time.

I was absolutely confused. How did this man who was surprised by automation, caught off guard by lights turning on, and impressed with the efficiency of a digital recording, have such a grasp of an electromagnetic safety rail system? In my attempt to rationalize the situation, I imagined my neighbor as a rather sheltered man who spent most of his time at the physics lab in Alabama he must have worked at, but otherwise not someone who got out very much.

* * *

It would have been nice to catch the 3:00 p.m. to Gatwick, but it was on a different airline and in the wrong terminal. I took the long, vaguely interiorly scenic, way back to terminal B. I took absolutely no notice of the moving sidewalk until I was struck with a sudden insight regarding my friend on the train. I mentally synched up with how, in part, he must see the world; as if waking up from a long sleep, that the world we lived in looked too much like a Jetson's cartoon to suit a reasonable man's sensibilities. Talking trains with robot voices, safety features based on principles of magnetism and radiation, automatic lights, moving sidewalks; the average international airport was Tomorrowland, and in general, probably all too cartoonish for its own good. Why don't we notice these things?

Coming to the conclusion that I had probably met the most reasonable man I was likely to meet that day, I kept walking back to Terminal B.

* * *

Any plane the size of a Boeing 777 will have at least four categories of seating. This is not always the rule. Sometimes you will find all four, or at least three, in smaller planes. But in a plane the size of a Boeing 777 you can always find all four. Typically, these will likely be conventionally labeled as: First Class, Business Class, Coach (or Economy) Class, and Ass.

Ass is designated not just in the last row of a Coach Class section, but specifically to those seats inaccessible once your neighbors sit down, such as those against a wall in the back row where the bulkhead meets the hull of the airplane. Features of Ass include not ever being able to recline your seat and probably having to share a window with the person in the row in front of you. Invariably, these passengers sharing the row with the passengers flying Ass will be the largest, surliest, and/or most brightly dressed people on the plane.

While flying Ass, expect to get your drinks first and never be served again. Place your trash in the seat pocket in front of you, because your cabin steward is not coming back.

It took seven hours for the Ass section of row 38, Coach, to decide collectively to go to the bathroom. Without consensus, it would never have happened.

Beverage carts scattered.

Considering the girth of our row, they had to. It was our only victory; we knew we would be last off the plane.

* * *

My meet-and-assist person did not meet or assist me upon deplaning. I don't normally ask for that kind of assistance, even when traveling internationally, and this is why. I had a choice, of course. I could have stuck around and asked, been directed, been redirected, and ultimately asked to wait some more, for this assistance to be dredged up. Or, I could just go and split the difference between efficiency and independence. Story of my life.

It isn't even that I need someone to read me the signs. It's just faster if they do. Having someone on the home team who knows the local rules and shortcuts is great. And of course, I'm shy, especially in crowds. That bit of ready made reluctance contributes to me being slow getting from New Point A to New Point B as much as anything to do with having trouble reading posted signs hung from the ceiling. I shouldered my bag and followed the departing crowd of passengers who had not flown Ass.

My subsequent journey through passport control, customs, and baggage claim was a disjointed relay race; spotting one sign after another and following arrows while trying to keep up with the American-looking (read: loud and impressed) passengers who were probably going the same way. I was now at large, and legal, in England.

I hitchhiked the crowds and signs to the Arrivals Terminal where crowds of lines crossed each other, intermingled, were broken by trolley caravans, and formed again like recombinating DNA decorated with little rolling black suitcases.

I circled for a few minutes before finding a line where the general consensus of the constituents was that I could get tickets to Heathrow on a shuttle bus. Nobody knew for sure, but everyone seemed comfortable enough with each other to risk spending a bus ride to Paris together if they were all wrong. It seemed like a win-win situation, so I went for it.

Not only was I sold a bus ticket to Heathrow, I was shown to a lounge slowly filling with Americans to catch the next shuttle. I don't book tours and don't travel in groups for the basic reason that I prefer to avoid Americans while overseas. In general, we are a loud, intense, opinionated, ignorant, and incongruously likeable mob that sees the purpose of an extended vacation to Europe to be an opportunity to visit America upon the Old World, one mid-western family at a time.

God bless us.

God save us.

Not to make me a liar, Fate placed on my shuttle a family from Dallas who spent the hour trip between airports complaining about British food, comparing their knowledge of British slang (for points, I think; it seemed to be a competition), and reminiscing about their favorite television programs back home. What few natives that had slipped onto these Americans' shuttle huddled in the back furtively waiting for their chance to make a break for it.

I shared a row with a woman on her way to Nairobi, Kenya, to participate in a conference to educate AIDS widows about their legal rights and practical options for daily living. She does this every year for two weeks- one in Nairobi, and one in western Kenya. She was not from Dallas, and therefore was not ranked in the British Slang Trivia competition going on by the luggage rack.

It also turns out she was in New York City on September 11th, 2001, and was, in fact, in the World Trade Center on September 10th. She described witnessing the events from across the river and how it felt to her like being trapped in a Stephen Spielberg movie. She went back to Ground Zero a couple months later, while on a business trip, to make it real for her, to dispel the cinematic magnitude of the memory for her. She was still working on it.

Imagine being in a bank. Without warning, armed gunmen storm in. They yell, they scream, they make demands and behave as armed gunmen are wont to do. They are criminals and in control of the situation. And then they shoot at you, but miss. Instead they kill the person standing next to you. There you go.

The family from Dallas was oblivious to our conversation. We did our best to be oblivious to theirs.

* * *

I chose Terminal 2 basically at random. If a person says they do something 'basically at random', this means a person may have good reasons for making bad choices. The problem arose in Dallas when they tried to check my bag through. An argument started between two airline personnel about whether or not my flight from Heathrow was Iberia or British Airways. The only answer I could get from them was a grudging, "It's both." This was a wonderful compromise that saved both of their egos but left my luggage in a quantum state.

Somewhere in the world right now is a hypothetical airline passenger named Schrodinger whose luggage will fly internationally on both of two potential airlines. Which airline it is will not be resolved until the passenger arrives at his destination and the luggage is lost, thus eliminating the quantum state while reinforcing Heisenberg's Uncertainty Principle of Connecting Flights Using Multiple Carriers.

At the shuttle counter back in Gatwick they insisted it was British Airways and that I'd get off at Terminal 2, not 4 which would be for Iberia. But, I just couldn't bring myself to get off the shuttle with the family from Dallas. This just seemed wrong. My shuttle companion had told me British Airways had flights leaving all four terminals. Terminal 2 was the next stop, so I disembarked the shuttle, with the Dallasians, against my better judgment, and made my way inside to get my bearings.

* * *

When we were being served breakfast on the plane, the pilot announced that we had entered British Airspace. I opened my window and was confronted with a general grey void pierced only by the dim green pulse from a wingtip. Judging by the impenetrable wall of fog I'd say yes, we definitely were over England. That's how the joke goes, right?

It didn't begin raining until I actually got off the bus though. I mean, to the second. For the two hours I'd been on the ground it had stayed grey and moist, but it didn't start being drippy, rainy wet until I had to be outside, bouncing between tube stops, bus stations, and finally the terminal; across the street and around the corner from where we were let off. That must be that British Sense of Humor I've always heard about. But there wasn't one damned dry thing about it.

* * *

Contrary to all previous commentary, Terminal 2 housed Iberian Air. The customer service counter and baggage check-in reached a consensus and it was determined that I was indeed in the right building. Or, at any rate, they were willing to fly me to Sevilla which amounted to pretty much the same thing.

* * *

I love traveling with Scottish Soccer Hooligans. If you ever have the opportunity to do so, do it. At least once. Think of it as a Bucket List thing. The farther they travel abroad from Scotland, the more like themselves they present themselves. It's sort of like watching tropical birds become defensive, throwing their crests up and puffing out their chests. It's not so much that they become comical as that they seem to intensify their colors and assert their dominance over the immediate territory. They do this by affecting a personality that is a seemingly incongruous mixture of charming Sean Connery-esque jewel thief and savage woad-daubed kilted madmen. They always respect the rules of the line at security, get the best service on airplanes, and are usually more entertaining than the in-flight movie.

In line to be x-rayed, I was behind two Scottish Soccer Hooligans. They were wearing casual business attire and carrying briefcase style satchels. But, despite their clever disguises, their cover was blown by the words "Glasgow Football Forever" tattooed in gothic lettertype on the backs of their shaved heads.

We moved through the checkpoint with no bother. While getting my things together I listened to the debate between the two security teams about which was better, line dancing or barn (square) dancing. As I was putting on my jacket I realized I had not taken off my boots. I love going through European Airport Security almost as much as traveling with Scottish Soccer Hooligans.

* * *

It is more difficult than you would think to buy a harmonica most places. In England, at least, this is probably due at least in part to the common slang term for the harmonica, the 'mouth organ'.

For the record: there is no place in Terminal 2's Departure Lounge to buy a harmonica. There are few places willing to discuss it. And there are only two women willing to offer advice about it. These two women are paid to give away samples of Armani cologne, and are very nice.

* * *

On the flight to Sevilla I sat next to Kim, a Dane working on an oil rig off the coast of Angola. He was on his way to the Canary Islands to see about purchasing a home for his weeks off.

Kim used to live in the United States, and enjoyed, in his time off, touring the Southwest in his motor home. He worked out of Long Beach, for a company that would pilot old oil rigs to the equator and launch commercial satellites from the floating platforms.

Now he's part of the marine crew on a rig off the African coast. Because it's a deep water rig with no permanent anchors, it is considered an ocean going vessel, and needs a ship's crew in order to operate in international waters.

Kim works four weeks on and four weeks off. There was currently a staff and crew of 149 men on his fifth generation rig. Its navigation system is thoroughly automated with satellite imaging, global positioning, multiple vector engines, and various redundant systems to keep the rig moving or stationary as necessary.

I tried hard not to think about the Jetsons, or sixth generation oil rigs sailing the open seas populated by robot' maids and talking dogs. I tried hard to be a reasonable man.

Of course, Kim explained, every automated system required multiple technicians, on site, to maintain operations. He said that he had worked on third generation rigs, that were considered almost obsolete now, that had a crew complement of 120 workers to do the exact same job as the rig he was working now.

He couldn't explain why the company would hire more workers on, to operate machines it had to pay to install, operate, maintain, and routinely upgrade, to get the same output as before. We decided the word he was looking for, in English, was "progress".

* * *

I slept most of the flight, missing the beverage service. I woke up in time to fill out my second immigration card of the day, having needed one to transfer from Gatwick to Heathrow.

I arrived in Sevilla and managed to get off the plane without any significant experience involving the bathroom, which made for a pleasant change of pace for the trip so far.

The airport in Sevilla, what I saw of it, was notable for having long ramps, longer large mirrors running the length of corridors, metal cages covering the ceiling and lights, and hardwood floors the color of a light pine. I had the distinct impression the place was designed purposefully in post-modern bowling alley.

* * *

Customs was so fun I went through twice. I had foolishly avoided the line for Citizens of the European Union and inadvertently declared myself a Citizen of Spain.

They were not fooled.

But, they were vaguely amused, and gave me a do-over. I went through the other line, apparently as an honorary European Unionite. Fortune favors the Bold. I was told I didn't need an immigration card. My paper was placed on a stack of other apparently unnecessary documents that had been collected that day, and I was waved through to baggage claim.

My bag was rolled up to me on the belt nearly as soon as I entered the next room. The luggage carousel was the type that meandered long and thin around the room until it disappeared into a hole in the wall, whisking unclaimed items off to Mister Rogers' Land of Make Believe.

* * *

Fernando met me outside the Avis rental office and informed me he had been waiting by the luggage belt for nearly an hour. My plane was late; that explained part of it. And, I had walked right past him holding his little sign and not seen him; that was the other part.

Fernando is that specific build of a man that the mind insists is egg shaped even when he's not. He is the style of man that runs very tan, is shorter than average, favors vests or v-necked sweaters, tends to wear spectacles, and always has a gohtee. Occupational trends for this type of man run along the lines of college professor, Buddhist monk, and surrogate father. Fernando came complete with a twinkle in his eye.

We drove to the train station where we picked up four other guests, and then we went to Epona.

* * *

I had been working under the impression that Epona was a small community outside of Sevilla. I was informed upon our tour of the grounds, that Epona referred

specifically to the Equestrian Center itself. Epona, the school, hostel, and vacation getaway, was named for the Celtic Goddess- a protector of horses- and operated as an officially recognized British Horse Society facility. While taking in tourists on a weekly

basis for riding lessons and horseback excursions into the countryside, the center operated a full time school for horse trainers as its primary function.

* * *

We met for dinner around 8:30 and were taken into town to dine and meet a sixth guest who would be staying with us for the week. On the way to the restaurant in Carmona, Fernando pulled off the side of the road at the gates of the old town center. Massive walls and towers rose into the night sky, marking the boundaries of the original historical community. Fernando explained as he took us past the open gates that the fertile Carmona valley used to be heavily forested, thriving with game as well as agriculture. There were ruins dug into the sides of some of the cliffs in the foothills dating back tens of thousands of years. There was also evidence of Greek and Phoenician settlement prior to Roman colonization. There was, in fact, enough archeological evidence to assert the claim that Carmona is the oldest perpetually permanently settled area in Europe.

As we were led briefly through Old Town, we saw huge metal portcullises held open for pedestrian traffic. We saw the bell towers where the peasants would be called in from the fields at night. We saw city streets, old and narrow, that did their best to wind around shops and buildings. We saw where the boiling oil would be mounted at the top of the walls, wall slits for archers to perch at, and the remains of a Roman dry moat that was built into the foundation of an outer wall. We saw layer after layer of wall, one built on top of the other, over thousands of years, rising above the city and the valley below.

* * *

A notice was posted above the toilet in my bathroom. It had a stop sign displayed prominently and bold letters requesting, "PLEASE THINK BEFORE USING THE TOILET". Before reading the rest of the notice and learning that it was an explanation of the center's septic system, I groaned softly at the realization that this had become something of a theme for my trip. And I had no idea exactly what to make of it.

* * *

Monday morning's ride took us through fields that were being sown with wheat and burned free of the last of the sunflower harvest. We rode through olive groves that were hundreds of years old. We rode for three hours, stopping halfway to let the horses graze and to rest ourselves. We were within sight of an abandoned hacienda that was being scavenged recently by locals for building materials. It was being taken apart

brick by brick and timber by timber over the course of months and years. It was over 500 years old.

* * *

Breakfast, lunch, and dinner were served in a cookhouse away from where we were lodged. Breakfast was continental, while the meals were served in courses: salad, entrée, and desert.

Breakfast was normally followed by a ride. Lunch was normally followed shortly be a lesson in the late afternoon. Dinner was at 8:00.

* * *

Tuesday morning Fernando drove us to Jerez to view a public demonstration by the Royal Andalusian School of Equestrian Art. We arrived early. Fernando purchased our tickets and we were tied to a coffee shop to wait for the gates to open. Fernando took the time to explain to us what we were about to see.

The Royal School trains horses, not people. This gets confusing. If an Andalusian colt is thought to be worthy to represent the breed at the Royal School, its owner contacts the director and the animal is measured to determine if it meets the breed's ideal physical characteristics. Then they are put through their paces to determine trainability. Finally, they must perform in fifteen public displays, such as what we were about to witness. If they proved to become collected and calm in front of the crowds then they will be purchased for an undisclosed price and kept until they are retired. This could be three months to a couple dozen years. They are then sold at public auction for breeding.

Here's when the Training of people creeps in. The riders in the first number of the demonstration, performed exclusively by the colts, are twelve of the sixteen human students at the school. Each student is apprenticed to a Senior Rider, four students per year for a four year term. Former students are the only applicants to be considered to become Senior Riders upon the retirement of a Senior Rider. Senior Riders have a job for life. They are considered Civil Servants, and pull down a six-figure income.

I did not ask if they were also sold to stud after they retired, but I suspect this may be the case.

Fernando's daughter, Vivi, was one of three female students at the Royal School. She was one of four applicants chosen out of over 75 in the final round of selection that year. She worked from 7:00 a.m. to 2:00 p.m. six days a week, and drove the one and a half hours to Jerez and back every day. She would probably be in the first number, but riders and horses were chosen secretly for each demonstration, so we wouldn't know till the show began if we would see her perform.

The second number would probably be a cowboy demonstration. The horses used by the Vaqueros are the only Andalusian cross breeds at the School. They are considered to be working horses, Fernando explained, compared to the high-action, collected stride of the pure breeds. These horses extend their legs and moved at a faster pace. To underscore this, the crosses were trained to not trot at all. They go from walk directly to canter,

Fernando explained again. In the United States, he surmised, it is likely that if you try to rope a bull and miss, it will continue milling around or wander away. In Spain… if you get the bull's attention and miss, it will come after you. And you'd better be able to move. Thus, the idea that the cross breeds, with their ability to go from first to third gear in a way the pure breeds can't, make for the better horses to take into the fields for work.

The remaining demonstrations would be a mixture of individual and group maneuvers and acrobatics with trainers on and off the horses.

No pictures would be allowed at the performance, but we could take photos of the riders warming up on the grounds. If we could find them. It seemed that most things at the school, in general, were very secret.

We finished our coffee and made our way back to the Royal School, with part of the group stopping to stick their heads into a tack shop we passed along the way.

* * *

Over the years Fernando had made friends with the Director of the Royal School. We picked randomly for our tickets, and I drew Row 1, Seat 1.

Before going into the performance, I took a quick look around the grounds of the school to see if I could find any of the students warming up. All I could find was two youngsters walking two surly Andalusians. Apparently, they weren't going to be in the show. The horses, I mean, which accounted apparently for their surliness.

We made our way inside.

My seat was near center at one end of the 20 meter by 80 meter exhibition area, just left of the Royal Box, which was unoccupied for this performance. To the right of the Royal Box the block of seats were occupied by a group of Japanese Tourists who were busy setting up tripods and adjusting shutter speeds. To say they were entrenched behind their equipment would only underscore the impression they made of setting up a machine gun nest that bristled with cameras instead of gun barrels. They would proceed to take pictures through the whole performance, contrary to the multilingual prohibition announced before the show over the stadium loudspeakers. One of my companions observed that since the announcement was only made in Spanish, English, and German, the stadium staff must have figured there was no stopping them.

The show commenced as Fernando predicted, being a full complement of demonstrations by the horses and trainers set to music. I saw dancing horses, racing carriages, the grace and power of a true vaquero, and precision riding- intricate, synchronized, and at speed- of beautiful horses ridden well. Amazing.

Not to downplay any of that at all, I need to go back to the racing carriages for a moment. Seriously, carriages. Like big fancy stage coaches rocketing back and forth through the arena. It was like a silent western on crack.

Somewhere in the world right now, a Japanese Tourist has all my pictures of the event, so you will have to believe me; it was amazing. Amazing.

* * *

Jerez is the center of the only region of the world where sherry, real sherry, is produced. As if to prove this, as if we were in any doubt, Fernando directed us to his favorite sherry shop, which was conveniently located just down the road from the Royal School.

Jamie stood out front performing various pouring tricks with a tiny ladle and several shot glasses. While inside, Antonio plied perspective customers with free samples and free advice about which sherry was right for them. It was very similar to going to a carnival booth and having your aura read.

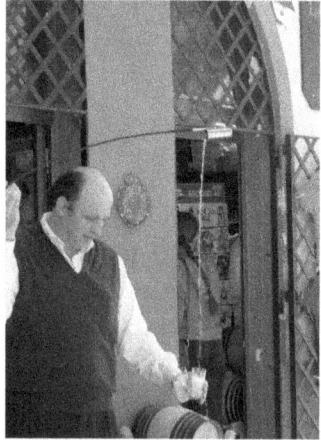

There are sherries you can have with breakfast. There are sherries you can have mid-morning. There are sherries you can have two hours before a meal (lunch or dinner), one hour before a meal, and sherries you should only have with your meal. There are sherries for desert, and sherries for after a meal, which are different. Pick a time of day, and Antonio could tell you the one or sometimes two, in those overlapping hours, specific sherries that you must have. He was fairly entertaining, thoroughly informative, and I'm almost positive subtly, and perpetually, drunk.

* * *

Earlier that day, on the way to Jerez, Fernando had pointed out to me a factory under construction just outside of Sevilla. He asked if I had ever heard of the Hercules Cargo Transport Military Aircraft. I indicated I had not, and he began to gesture grandly to indicate the size of the thing. "Huge," he said, "massive." He grabbed the wheel again and continued.

I enjoyed riding up front with Fernando because he usually had something to point out and talk about. The trick was keeping him as interested in driving as he was excited about sharing.

The European Union was building their own version of the Hercules via consortium. The new plane would sport a Rolls-Royce engine, German Cockpit, Italian wings, all built and shipped to Sevilla for assembly from their company of corporate origin. This meant 15,000 jobs, and 150 skilled technical jobs would be created to put the planes together for the European Union's army.

I was not aware the European Union had an army.

Oh yes, I was informed, they were in the process of standardizing all the weapons and armor so that soldiers from any country could operate the machines and armament of any other country. For instance, the German Leopard tank would be the standard pattern battle field tank for the European Union armored infantry.

I wondered how this concept fit together with a consortium driven assembly line. I also wondered dully exactly who Europe planned to be at war with where open-source knowledge of the technical specifications of all their military hardware by other European nations would be an asset and not a liability. If I remembered my history right, Europe only really had experience with being at war with itself; except for all those times countries in the Americas revolted. Then again, I figured, Europe had had enough experience with running wars By Committee that it was not my place to be critical.

* * *

On our way from the coffee shop to the Royal School, Fernando had overheard a discussion in the group about saddles. He informed us that he only, ever, rode a McClellan saddle. It was not good for dressage, nor was it a true English saddle. However, he could find no better saddle for trail riding or cross country 'hacking'.

He told us to look in the common room at the center when we got back, where he had a McClellan saddle on display. A friend of his from Wyoming sent it to him. The friend was a history buff, and heavily interested in civil war reenactments. While rooting through an old barn one day, which I guess is something people in Wyoming do when not participating in Civil War reenactments, he found eight saddles, of which this was one. They all dated to the last half of the 1800's.

I saw the saddle when we returned. Vintage. It was a true museum piece. Found in a barn. And sent overseas through the mail.

* * *

My afternoon lessons during the week consisted of trying to make a horse trot without slowing to a walk, while I managed to look convincingly upright. The horse occupied her time during these lessons by breaking consistently into a walk from a trot, and trying her best to manage to drive me convincingly forward, or possibly off. We never quite managed to oblige each other.

* * *

Fernando rode with us on Wednesday morning's hack. Business and operation of the center had kept him from joining us in the country until then, but he was a horse person and wanted to be out there with us on our ride.

(My fellow guests were all Horse People, and by strange and unrelated coincidence, all lived on islands. The family of three was from Victoria, British Columbia. The other two ladies, Wendy and Vicky, were from The Isle of Man and the Canary Islands, respectively. I was picking up all sorts of lingo like "collection", "lead", and "diagonal", none of which have sensible definitions.) (But I lived in the desert and am not, technically, a Horse Person. So, what do I know?)

We rode down the dirt road, out through the open fields, and turned down a track about four feet wide bordered by grass on both sides which ran between fields and groves. Fernando explained: In this part of Andalusia

you could travel for days without touching asphalt or pavement. Horses were such a part of the culture that they had right of way on the tracks between fields as well as across those fields that were unplanted. Because we could travel along these tracks between conventional dirt roads and pathways, tracks you might actually find on a road map of the area, there was essentially an infinite number of horse trails in Andalusia.

Furthermore, he continued, "unlike in some countries where there is more lawyers than citizens, if you or your horse gets hurt on the farmer's land, you don't sue him and he doesn't sue you. Everyone knows this is an accident. They understand horses here. The farmers, they love to see horses riding through the fields. The horse is part of the culture here. If someone gets hurt, no one blames anyone, except maybe the horse." He did not elaborate about whether the horse would be the accuser or accusee when it came to assigning blame. I could see it going either way.

We rode through fields, olive groves, and citrus orchards till we reached an estate in the middle of the plain with very loud, very cautious dogs in the front yard. We turned down a tree-lined path and then cut away into the edges of the first truly wild forest growth we had encountered that week. We forded a stream and walked through to a clearing as Fernando pointed out the Roman bridge.

The bridge had been there for over a thousand years. As the horses grazed, a hare broke from the bushes and tore through the grove, and disappeared into the forest. The horses continued eating, paying no attention to the bridge or the hare.

* * *

According to Fernando, Sevilla was the birthplace of the Roman Emperors Hadrian and Trajan, and the Roman Governor Pontius Pilot. Pilate was nicknamed for his prowess with the short javelin, or pilota. (The more common name in Latin is 'pilum', and the weapon was typically five feet of wooden shaft tipped with about two feet of iron.) According to Fernando, our resident guide and Good Son of Andalusia, Pilate was literally named Pontius Pilota, Pontius "the Lance". Local tradition holds that he was revered as an athlete, and warrior, before entering into civil service.

* * *

Our ride Wednesday morning was steadily punctuated alternately by my cursing and application of what my instructor referred to as, "a *proper* kick". My trail horse, Kahlua, refused to match pace with the horse in front when we were riding in pairs, and it was all I could do to move him into a trot on cue. It typically took the combined weight of the other horses riding single file up his backside to make him lengthen his stride. He did not canter, which was just as well,

since cantering had not been covered yet, though I had

been told that it might be covered in that afternoon's lesson.

* * *

It was not. My designated instructor had the day off and I spent the afternoon's lesson trying to prod Walkeria, my lesson horse, into a consistent trot while rising and sitting to the beat of various bone-jarring rhythms set by my surrogate trainer. Balance and leg position figured in there too, somewhere, but I can't remember. Pain makes you forget sometimes.

* * *

Thursday morning we drove an hour and a half, past the town of Rosio on the Atlantic coast, to the stables of Don Antonio. We drove past marshland reserve where 4,000 wild horses reside. We drove through Piñon forests where pine nuts are harvested. We drove through a town where every public building and place of business had a hitching post outside.

The funny thing about pine nuts is that they must be harvested before the cone falls from the tree. The green cones are fired to open and then the nuts can be collected. But, if the cone has matured there will be no nuts inside to harvest. They are so expensive because they must be picked by hand. The Dr. Seuss-like dandilion-esque trees have branches that can only be accessed by a ladder, and are typically too high to be wacked at with even the longest of sticks.

Don Antonio stabled only pure-bred Andalusians. We mounted up on his property and were taken into the surrounding Humanitarian Nature Preserve where we would ride for three hours round trip to the beach and back. The only access to the park was on foot or on horseback, and Don Antonio's stable was across the street from a park entrance. Location, location, location.

From the second highest peak in the preserve we could see the Atlantic Ocean on one side, peaceful, with a shrimp boat working its way slowly out in the distance. On the other side, stretching away beyond as far as the others could see, was the preserve. The park was first established by the Spanish government, then perpetuated by the European Union as a haven to conserve and protect endangered species native to the coast. The only buildings we could see, the only buildings on the property, Fernando told us, were research facilities, classrooms and study centers, and the hunting lodges of the Spanish nobility.

We rode Spanish saddles for the ride through the park. They were wide and stiff, with a reinforced curb of a backrest and the proto-form of a saddle horn in the front. They were also, and this is important, covered in sheepskin. Not a wool pad. The skin of a sheep. (This is the difference between lying on a grassy hillside in the middle of summer and sitting on a straw mat in a dusty barn.) Being used to riding horses much bigger than the Andalusians back in the states, the broader width of the saddle on the tiny purebred put my legs into a comfortable position on the horse for the first time all week. With the thick layer of wool to boot, it was like riding a well-trained cloud down the trails to the beach.

I could write more by way of comparison about riding English or McClellen saddles on the smaller horses at Epona. But after I had used up words like bony, stubborn, chaffing, and devil-horse, there may not be too many words left fit to print. I take part of the blame for not being a good enough rider for the horses, those smug, fancy Equestrian Center horses, to respect. But only that part of the blame.

My companions, as I've mentioned before, were all Horse People. They spoke horse, owned horses, played horse, and trained horse. I, am not, technically, a horse person. I trail ride. I take lessons. I like to ride on vacations. And, I don't speak horse. To be as they are around horses would be like for me, as one of the last clowns out of the tiny car, to take suddenly to the trapeze.

Back at Epona, for the past several days, I had been riding horses so well trained that they know exactly how to take advantage of a novice rider and do as little as possible under that rider's direction. Imagine my surprise to find myself astride an animal, conversely so well trained, that it did what it was told and seemed happy to do it. I was able to apply leg aids, as I understood the term, to direct the horse and/or adjust our speed. The reins, if used at all, required a feather touch. After nearly a week, I actually rode a horse that didn't make me feel stupid. It was like learning a new language and successfully ordering your first beer in a foreign country.

* * *

On the beach we fanned out and found a stretch of hard packed sand. Fernando announced that we were going to canter. Then, he remembered himself, and asked if I wanted to canter as well. Want to? Yes. Was I expecting to? No. Was I up for it? Well, the sand looked soft, so sure.

We, my fellow tourists and I, clustered. A few offered advice, most of which involved keeping my heels down. And not falling off. That one came up a couple times too. We were instructed to line up and ride in order, single file.

When the canter hit, and it hit like a wave driving the horses forward from behind, we immediately fanned out again, hauled our respective asses, and only really took care to not pass Don Antonio. (None of us wanted to get into trouble.)

It wasn't like flying. It was like being flown. It wasn't like sailing. It was like being the sail.

Over the years of taking riding lessons I had been taught many things. I applied them as the situation demanded. I dropped my heels. I kept my back straight. I held my shoulders back. I gripped with my calves, not my knees. I did not fall off.

Damn. So *that's* what it was like.

I don't think I stopped running till after my nap that afternoon.

* * *

I woke up with a sore back. A cramped shoulder that was getting started on the ride back to Don Anonio's stable had blossomed in my sleep into a potpourri of pain across my upper back. That's what good posture gets you.

I spent the majority of my lesson that afternoon walking and talking with my instructor. It turns out we had the same birthday, and she liked really bad movies (too). When I did trot near the end, I felt more relaxed, and Walkeria and I both made a good show of ourselves at the end of the day.

* * *

Friday morning's ride was out to a stud farm a couple hours' ride away. I spent most of the time riding next to my afternoon instructor, Toni, in the back, and talking about the best and worst science fiction movies we had ever seen, and what we wanted to be when we grew up.

She was from Norway and about ten years younger than me. I probably should have offered advice. I probably should have been in a position to offer advice. I offered sympathy.

Toni pointed out to me an abandoned dairy farm a few fields over. As per European Union environmental regulations, the Spanish government had banned dairy farming in the south of Spain because there wasn't enough grass to support the industry. Then the Spanish government bought up all existing dairy farms. This one was in the process of being turned into an olive oil processing facility.

That made sense.

* * *

We rode on.

The day was pleasant. The sky was blue. The wind picked up just enough to make the air cool again. We rode down a riverbed, much to my chagrin, because of my fear of water, and to Toni's dismay, because she was a leggy woman on a small horse.

I have been visiting Arizona for twelve years now, and living in Tucson for the last eight. When someone says to me the word 'riverbed', I think of dry, wide stretches of sand where water, according to historians, once flowed through Tucson. I have to remember that nearly everywhere else in the world 'riverbed' means the place at the bottom of the river. Under the water. Because rivers have water in them. Not like in Tucson.

So I am being specific here, to avoid ambiguity. In case anyone is reading this who might be living n Tucson. We were following the river from the center while the water rolled along with us high enough to make the difference between us swimming and us walking a matter of negotiating semantics.

While still in the saddle, she shortened her stirrups and rode it out with her legs up like a jockey. Her knees were not quite up around her ears, but if I had to draw a cartoon of it there would definitely be a frog like aspect to the caricature.

* * *

At the stud farm we saw mares far out in the fields and foals corralled in their own enclosure. We took a break, letting the horses graze, and minding to keep them away from the electric fence. We set out again through the paths between fields.

While riding earlier that morning, one of my companions riding near the front found his horse overtaking the rider in front of him at the canter. We were instructed that, were this to happen, we were to turn our animal into the back of the beast in front of us, the horses being trained properly not to run each other down. This is the difference between horses and, say, ostriches. Horses have to be properly trained to not run each other down.

Instead, my fellow guest took the horse out and away into the fields, slowing it down with ever tightening circles until it was brought to a walk in the turned soil. This is the difference between horses and, say, people. Upon being properly trained they follow their training. By comparison, it takes a man to be a cowboy. Horses aren't free thinkers that way.

Our leader on the trail that day was a Horse Person. Not a cowboy. The display of independent problem-solving in the face of training upset our guide. Our guide's agitation, in turn, set the rest of the group on edge. The horses remained hot for the rest of the morning.

Halfway back to Epona, we decided to canter one last time. It was an extended stretch between fields, turning as it met a service road that led into an olive orchard.

We lined up in single file, moved into a posting trot, and prepared to canter out. Kahlua was awake, finally, after a week. He launched forward on cue, his legs extending on canter, in complete, infuriatingly complete, contradiction to the high action of his grudging trot. With an intelligence born from his need for speed, my horse began to work his way around and down the line. I dutifully brought him in line with the Andalusian in front of me.

That's when it began.

Instead of slowing his canter, my horse shifted to a high, fast, trot. The rolling gait, the smooth stretching run, turned suddenly into an upthrusting jog that carried me up and forward as he broke speed. My body tilted. My legs clenched, but slipped.

Kahlua had shed enough speed with this maneuver to give him the room to go around and down the line in earnest. After a weeks worth of walking I still don't know how he managed to pass cantering horses at a trot, but damned if he didn't have it in him.

By the time we passed the first horse, I was over Kahlua's neck. My fingers were twisted between reins and mane. At this point I noticed my feet were not in the stirrups anymore. Snapshots of reality were slamming into me over five seconds of eternity as I processed the horse taking control.

People had shouted. I know this because I was one of them. I think I said something clever like, "Nooo, whoahhh, #%@$^ stop!" Other people said other, more clever things that were slowing the line down. Toni, riding hard, was running up behind me outside the line. Kahlua rode on, drove forward. My heart beat once, a distinctive lub-dub that ticked away another interval in my life.

And then the scene shifted.

It was like the world was edited in the cutting room of my life. The camera of all my senses turned off and refocused on a perspective that had been switched to meet the script.

I was riding at canter. My back was straight, shoulders back, reins between my last three fingers in each hand, held two fists apart over the pommel of the saddle. Steady pressure brought the rolling strides into a sitting trot, and then a walk, and then a halt that pawed the ground. My seat was firm. My contact with thighs and calves was as near to perfect as I've ever managed. I felt right riding that horse down under control.

It was when I had halted that I realized my feet were still out of their stirrups.

Don't ask me how I did it. I won't be able to tell you.

Toni, God bless her, caught up, riding circles around me to slow her horse down and pen Kahlua in. Just in case. She asked if I wanted to walk and trot, letting the group ride on. I declined. She asked if I wanted to canter ahead with just her and have the group catch up. Once I caught my breath, I said yes. She informed the trail guide while I collected myself.

We rode.

Faster than I had ever felt before.

Like wind. Like fire. Like heat. Like being pulled. Like being carried on will. Like being taken through the air.

The horses raced. Not quite at a gallop, they rode side by side, pushing one in front of the other, taking turns in the lead. We both had to lean on the reins hard to bring them down before we entered the olive groves just down the track and around the bend.

* * *

It was the end of the olive harvest. Workers made their way through the orchards with long-poled instruments designed to beat the branches and bring down the last, clinging vestiges of the crop.

They were like sticks, but since they were tools they had a name. I never did learn what they were called but never felt right just calling them sticks. Because they were tools. That sort of thing matters.

Depending on when they are picked, olives will be green or black. At this time of year, nets, like upside-down umbrellas, were spread out under the ancient trees to catch the last tender blacks as they fell to close the season.

* * *

Friday night saw us to Sevilla for shopping and a flamenco performance. El Caballo- purveyor of fine clothes and tack was open after six in the evening and played host to our group as we picked through scarves, spurs, and saddles. While one of our number was being measured for custom fittings on a new set of half chaps to fit over a smashing new pair of boots and britches, I received an education on the various ways a horse could be brutalized by bit and bridle as a few of us examined the array of metal bars and chains strung across one section of wall.

I picked through books with pictures of horses and many Spanish words. I flipped through DVDs that wouldn't play in any North American DVD machine. In the end, I bought a scarf. There was no language barrier to overcome, and I didn't need to buy any adapters to make it run without exploding.

We walked to El Patio De Sevilla, where we were greeted by the proprietor. Fernando peeled us into groups based on how we were paying. People with Euros took precedence over those using other currency.

The theater was a medium-sized hall arranged around and away from the front of the stage. A balcony level ringed the main floor. We were escorted to where Fernando had reserved our seats, second row center, and were served our complementary beverage.

Sevilla is the birthplace of Flamenco. First came the dance. Then, the instrumental. And finally, the voice.

The cadence and punctuation of the dancers stepping time was wrapped in the rattlesnake rhythms of the castanets. The strumming of the guitar was the vibrations of racing heartbeats and autumn winds. The voice of the singer filled the hall with a thick honey that fell around us like the sorrow of angels.

The performance of an homage to Carmen seemed obligatory, yet appropriate. It was placed in the program like the Our Father- required to conclude the liturgy, requisite prior to the Eucharist.

The troupe continued in solo, dual, and group performances. They were joined by a beautiful young woman in a brown dress, who was not as good as the other female dancers, but I didn't care. She was in nearly every number for the last half of the show.

Most of us congregated in the lobby afterward and waited for Fernando and the other guests to come out. Fernando joined us after speaking with the proprietor and the members of the troupe. Like the trip to Jerez to see the Royal School, Fernando had been to El Patio nearly every Friday for the last several years. He was Known.

I ceased my examination of the great bull's head in the lobby and walked with my group down mosaic tile sidewalks. Out group, those who purchased items from El Caballo they did not feel like wearing to the recital, were now burdened with sundry bags of chaps and tack delivered discretely to the concert hall during the performance. I, unburdened, wore my scarf.

We made our way to the restaurant where we were seated in the rear, where it was warm. Fernando was greeted warmly and by name by the owner and the staff as they laid out salads and plates of olives. Fernando was amused by the face I pulled as I ate my first olive, ever. When in Rome... I liked it. But, it was very strong and not quite like anything I had ever eaten before. Fernando was bemused.

He explained: during the civil war food was short. Many people, all they had to eat was an olive, smashed into a paste, and spread over bread. That may be all they had to eat all day. You eat what you have to.

I ate three more olives before ordering.

* * *

Upon harassing revelations by my companions, Fernando learned of my infatuation with the woman in the brown dress. He offered me her phone number.

I declined. I was in town for one more day. What would I do calling her, speaking English, leaving the country? Then I decided he couldn't be serious.

So of course he pulled out his address book, tapped a page with a fingernail, and said, "Too bad. Inga is very nice." Then his book, and my fantasy, slipped back into his coat pocket.

I ate venison, fish from my neighbor's plate, two more olives, and a desert I can't spell.

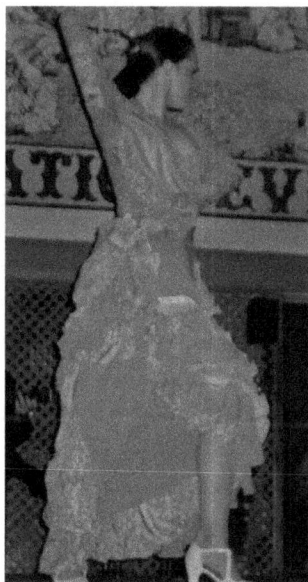

Fernando told us that Inga was an understudy. He said that the woman who played Carmen fell during the intermission, hurt her knee, and was rushed to the hospital.

* * *

I did not sleep that night.

I packed, stretched, took a hot shower. I wrote, stared at the ceiling, and finished a book. I cleaned my room, and joined my fellow guests for our last breakfast.

* * *

It was decided that I would travel with the majority of the guests into Sevilla at 9:30. I had been planning to say my goodbyes at the train station, make my way to the hotel, and pass my time in the city. By the time I had reached the airport, where the family was departing to secure a rental car, I had received one offer to meet the family group and their friends for the horse show in the afternoon and a flamenco performance in the evening, and another invitation to join my remaining companion for the horse show that morning.

And so, rather than moving from train station to hotel for a brief nap and a tour of the city, a convoluted plan was developed that entailed sharing cabs and buying tickets for the horse show, and checking luggage at a train station I wouldn't be departing from (apparently you can do that). Fernando agreed, for his part, to extend his service to us in the form of a trip to the train station and a ride to the horse show. My companion, Vicky, who was from England but lived in the Canary Islands, agreed to act as translator and guide. I agreed to go along with it all. And so, Fate conspired with my dazed indifference to keep me awake a little longer.

* * *

Fernando parked in the circle where he stopped to pick up the other guests a week before. He stayed with the minivan while my companion and I searched for the luggage check office.

At a sub-level, around the corner from a loading dock, we found a small, black door set in a stone wall. Inside was low-ceilinged, stretched perspective, where dim incandescent bulbs near the front fought with flickering fluorescent bulbs in the roof for blame over which was the true source of the gloom and dusty shadows. If there was more glare the space would not seem so faded, or scuffed.

Brief inquiries at a counter manned by an indifferent uniformed gentleman who gestured more than he spoke propelled us through a security check point where our bags and luggage were x-rayed and we were metal-detected. We were turned through hallways into corridors of lockers where we would check our things.

A circular depression on each locker was crossed by a bar grip that turned on a central axis. Opening the lockers provided the expectation of a hiss and the release of pressurized steam. I half-anticipated that the drawer would slide towards me at the end of a drawer containing some vital serum or deadly isotope. With a click that sounded like 'click', the door swung open on hinges.

It was deep enough inside to handle all my luggage and carry-on bags. I had paid to open the locker, and received a printed ticket from a keypad terminal in-between blacks of doors. This only reinforced earlier fantasies; no retina scanner though. Returning with the code printed on the ticket would release my contents before heading back to the hotel after the show. All I had to do now was find my way back to the parking lot.

* * *

Before getting back in the car we checked in with Fernando and went around to the front of the station where the public transportation was. Vicky and I fussed over the bus schedule for about ten minutes, trying to decide whether the numbers listed were times for arrival at the airport, or departure from the train station. In the end, we just took note of the times and the fact that they ran at regular half-hourish intervals, and returned to the van.

My faith in Vicky as an interpreter was only slightly diminished. To be fair, there were more numbers than words on that sign, and numbers can mean anything.

It was about half after ten in the morning, and we would have to return between six and seven for my companion to get to the airport in time for her flight. I was supposed to check into my hotel by 4:00. I was told to relax, as if the prospect of staying the night on the streets of Sevilla was nothing they had to worry about.

* * *

SICAB 2004 – The Salon Internacional de Caballo de Pura Raza Española – was the international horse show of international horse shows. I had been hearing about it all week from the guests at Epona. Sevilla had swelled with Horse People. More importantly, to the back of my mind, the hotels of Sevilla had swelled with Horse People. It was the final day of the show, and Sevilla was ecstatic with pride, culture, tourism, and general horsiness.

Fernando had missed Friday morning's ride because he had been invited to SICAB with friends visiting from Hungary. He was on his way back now, and was willing to shuttle us because he had purchased a print for his wife and needed to pick it up. He prepared us for the experience as we wound through the streets of Seville.

Thousands of people from southern Spain and across Europe would be there. Only slightly less would have been there Friday morning when Fernando went. This made for crowding and noise and excitement, all about horses and all things to do with horses.

And business. Fernando said it was not so much about shopping as it was about doing business. The Salon boasted a bar, a sit-down restaurant, another less expensive eatery, and any number of vendors and stalls so the crowds would never go hungry or thirsty. "In Spain," he explained, "all business is done with a glass in the hand." My mind was filled with visions of a European Union defense contract for the production of cargo jets that had wobbly signatures at the bottom.

* * *

There were crowds.

Well dressed Sevillans filled the plaza. Mounted officers flanked the entrance to the grounds. A mob organized itself outside the ticket windows. Knots of people filled the rotunda outside the exhibition halls.

There was a brief empty space of noise and people between the Information Commons in the rotunda and the Central Hall. Then, cacophony personified in Legion.

Crowd implies tightness, but leaves hope of space to breathe. This was bigger. The central exhibition hall was corridored with carpet to keep the stalls from stretching into each other as they tried to pour out onto the pedestrian throughways. Being eddied into the shops gave you an opportunity to inhale and stretch your limbs for enough movement to sort coats or scarves or hats or breeches. Saddles- dressage, English, Spanish, Vaquero, and Portuguese- were displayed on the fanciest of cat trees. (It occurred to me that an entire industry was created around building racks to display saddles on at horse shows. Then I wondered, how would you express that on a business card?)

We spent the better part of the morning being drifted around the hall. At one point, we found ourselves at the rear of the hall where an eighty meter arena was installed and competitions were commencing throughou the day. We crowded against a rail and looked over shoulders at young vaqueros putting horses through their paces. The crowd blocked the extremities of the arena, and it was easier to try to stand still against the jostling and watch the jumbo screen TV at the near corner than to attempt to keep track of what was going on in the ring.

We separated briefly, arranging to meet near one of the exits, and I spent most of the intervening time swimming upstream past stalls selling prints, jewelry, leather creams, and horse-related videos. I spent about five minutes swirling around in the tidal pool of people in front of the hall doors until I was rescued by my companion and pulled out to look at vests and helmets.

Come mid-afternoon, we began wading through bleachers between performances back at the arena, in hopes of finding a place to sit. Watching the next exhibition would be a happy side effect of our mission, but by that point in the day our primary objective was to not be standing anymore.

We were lucky to find seats in the same row, though we were not next to each other. Space was tight. Some inner travel reflex kicked in, as if I was flying coach, and I finally went to sleep, there in the stands.

My dreams were scented with hay and cotton candy. To be fair though, by that point in the day, so was I. There was no sequence to the visions of memory, no story to my dreams, only vague recollections of tap dancing horses and classical music. In my dream, the crowds around me were Asian, not Spanish. This would mean I had traveled home in my sleep to California. At least then, the image I had of Zorro flying around the ring on a black Andalusian colt would have made more sense.

I am generally critical of my dreams for lacking an alien quality of the fantastic. Typically, they may be non-linear, non-causal, and full of non-sequiturs. But the symbols and images I'm left with from my nap at SICAB were that much more beyond identification or ready interpretation. Clearly too many fumes from hay and cotton candy had taken their toll.

Vicky and I climbed, literally, out of the stands and exited the hall for some air. The three exhibition halls fanned out from the rotunda like rays from a rising sun. We found that the spaces between the halls were filled with horse stalls for the animals that would be competing. The horses with window views of the crowds ranged from surly to timid to petting zoo friendly. Trying to decide which was which held the potential for danger. One horse finally just gave up and laid down to go to sleep. The stalls inside the first hall were less energetically populated. The horses kept inside the hall were listless and prone to angry stares. The far hall was dominated by a massive competition ring and bleachers.

We swung past a specific stall selling videos for the fifth time that day. The modem on the visa reader was still not working, so Vicky could not purchase her Olympic comemerrative DVD highlighting the Equestrian competition. We would come back again later and it still wouldn't be working. She would settle for a calendar and some prints as her trophies for the day's ordeals, before we went back to the train station.

Consulting the schedule, we fought our way to the farthest exhibition hall from us, where a new show was supposed to be starting. While the crowds weren't as dense as in the central hall's stands, we still had to look for seats next to each other, and those were only available near the doors. We waited for the next competition to begin. What was happening when we arrived was a series of exhibitions from contestants who had won earlier competitions. I fell asleep, again.

Vicky let me doze next to her for about half an hour. Afterward, we split a couple of sandwiches and headed back to the train station, after one more sweep through the main hall.

* * *

We shared a taxi to the train station where we said our goodbyes after retrieving our belongings from the dungeon underneath. My companion went inside to an information desk to confirm that we had missed one of her buses by five or twenty five minutes. I never did figure out which, and neither corresponded to our hypothetical formulas for the bus schedule we thought we were looking at before going to the Salon. We were assured by everyone, from the information booth man to the random passersby glancing at the posted numbers, that another bus would be along in another five to twenty five minutes. Again, this did not correspond with any table-reading mechanics or strategies I was employing. I had to assume the numbers meant different things in Europe, or, maybe the schedule was a suggested guideline. Or, maybe everyone was just guessing.

* * *

I kissed her twice, once on each cheek (as was the fashion), and we said goodbye. The taxis were pulled up on the other side of the island from the bus stop. I went to the front of the line of cars and headed to my hotel. It was now 6:30, and I hoped they had held my reservation.

I knew, from the efforts of other guests staying at Epona, that hotel rooms were hard to come by that weekend due to SICAB. My travel agent wouldn't have known this when I had booked the trip that summer. Considering how far in advance I had booked, she may not have had any reason to learn it.

Regardless, I had no idea what kind of accommodations I had secured. (You can't always tell from a picture of a queen size bed next to a tasteful set of chairs.) (Or a writing desk, as the case may be.). My misgivings (read: fantastic imaginations) were only fueled by my agent's report that I had been booked in a place called "The Silken Owl". From the time she had told me this, I could not shake the impression that I was going to Spain and spending my last night there in a Texas Bordello. As time went by, before the trip, I made a point of calling and confirming the name. Yes, I was told, The Silken Owl. But I shouldn't worry, it was a four star establishment. Well, okay then, I thought to myself, I'm going to Spain and spending my last night there at a Texas Bordello with cable, a hot tub, air conditioning, room service, sauna, and a weight room.

Accents can be a funny thing. Once while in college, my ex-wife reported, there was an incident where a young undergrad from Oklahoma interrupted her Western History lecture with the question, "How d'ya spell Pau?"

Everyone was confused except the professor, who was also from the Sooner State. He responded off-handedly, in his best Norman Oklahoma nasal pitch, "P O dubya E L L," and continued his discussion without missing a beat.

My travel agent, whom I love dearly, in an affectionately Travel Agent's client kind of way, was a native of the city of Tucson. It is easy to forget that Tucson has native-born citizens, considering how rapidly it has grown in the past thirty years. But it does, and at the core of the hearty population lies the Spirit Of Tucson.

It is a city that calls dry trenches rivers. It is a city that hasn't come to grips with its size or its century. It is a city that hasn't realized it has become a metropolis, and can stop struggling to be a frontier town. It is a city so steeped in obscure yet addictive history that its culture has permeated the spoken word.

The resident Tucsonan, native or otherwise, is most likely to pronounce Grande, "grandee". Tanque

Verde becomes "taynkuh verdee". And, Tohono O'otham, the name of the local Native American Tribe whose reservation is the second largest in the country, is reduced on the Anglo tongue to "T. O.". It is meant as a compliment; an awkward embrace from an affectionate distant cousin.

And so it was, bless her heart, that my travel agent checked me in to the Hotel Silken Al Sevilla. I do not know what Al means. It is possible that, in Spain, it means Owl. I would rather not ever find out.

* * *

The hotel, one of the Silken (to rhyme with 'Hilton') chain of hotels, was big and bright and full of glass walls and shiny floors. I picked my way carefully to the front desk, following the doorman who offered to carry my bags. When I tipped him two euros, he guarded my luggage viciously while I checked in, and carried everything up to my room for me when I got my keys.

The hallways flowed past like I was sliding down a long tube that ended at the bed in my hotel room. I woke up several hours later and called my companions who had invited me to the flamenco performance and let them know I wouldn't be meeting them at the horse show that evening but that I would try to make the performance. I fell asleep again as the handset hit its cradle.

I woke again, aware I did not have the wherewithal to go out anymore. The idea of noise and crowds and being social with friendly strangers overwhelmed me. I called their cell phone again and apologized. I thanked them for their generous invitation. Then I took a hot bath.

* * *

I was brought around by my wake up call. Repacking was a minimal effort, and checking out, a formality. My ride to the airport probably cost more than it should have, I don't recall taking the freeway on any of the routes I'd taken within the city to date. I had to take out money from a machine to cover the fare, which was fine because I would have Euros on hand against a falling dollar when I came back into the States.

I stepped boldly to the Iberia Air counter and presented my British Airways ticket without shame. As the gentleman checked my bags through to Tucson, I studied the picture diagram of items you could not bring in your carry-on bags. I noticed they had added forks to the standard list of knives and scissors and shivs.

I was directed down the counter and around the corner to security. Passage was easy. For the second time on my trip I kept my boots on in the face of uniformed guards.

I walked past gift shop after gift shop that was closed. Apparently Sunday morning was not the time to shop for souvenirs at Sevilla International. I set up at a coffee shop for breakfast and listened for my gate to be announced.

When the call came I made my way to the line for the passport control outside Gate 1. Behind me in line were two young women who were loud and in a state of constant disbelief about how inconvenient the world could be.

Once, while studying in London, I was riding the tube with my roommate when a bunch of Texans got into our car. After being loud for a while, and informing everyone in earshot about how terribly inconvenient they found the world to be, one of them laughed and said, "Hey, y'all know that everyone in this train's thinkin' 'f**kin' 'mericans?'" Matt and I looked at each other and he nodded, reading my mind. "Yup," he said out loud, "That's exactly what we're thinking."

I looked over my shoulder as my passport was stamped.

You said it buddy.

* * *

They did not stop talking while we waited to board. They did not stop talking while our boarding passes were checked. I do not believe they stopped talking the whole way to Heathrow. I could be wrong. The noise from the back of the plane could have been two other people having a highly intelligent debate about the role of humanitarian aid organizations in the third world in the face of volatile political climates. But, just in case it wasn't, I focused on my bag of peanuts and tuned the whole thing out.

Captain Rodriguez seemed to have missed out in a career training horses. He flew his plane like a stallion that needed to be broken. Flying was a point and go affair for him. The approach to Heathrow is where he shined. Turns were turns, not gentle arcs or sweeping banks. He thrashed the sky like an arrogant surfer. He rode through the terrain of the wind like it was so much irrelevant underbrush. His landing was a controlled dive under power. Touchdown was perfect. The problem of slowing down was solved by, near as I could tell, the engines decelerating to null speed for an instant, then reversing. The whole thing was smooth, like riding a Tiger on a silk saddle.

* * *

Transit from the Gate at Heathrow to the departure lounge was a winding circuit through empty halls and back stairs. At first I crept along from sign to sign, avoiding passport control and security, confident I would not be entering the country. Eventually I fell in behind a middle-aged couple arguing about what gate the flight to Phoenix was leaving from. I hitchhiked behind them mindlessly until they broke left of a set of velvet ropes. The man went to the right of a pillar; the woman turned left. I took two steps into the Ladies' Room before spinning on my heel, ducking under the ropes, and heading the rest of the way on my own.

* * *

I did, as it turned out, have to go through security again. I made it through, yet again, with my boots on, but they insisted on unpacking my carry-on. At this point, Heathrow security confiscated my fork.

I make no apologies for having one in my bag. A fork can be a very handy thing. To be honest though, I had forgotten it had been in my bag until I had reviewed the diagram in Sevilla. I reasoned, however, that since my fork had gotten into Europe without raising alarm, officials would be just as happy to let it out without comment. I was wrong, and now my fork lives an exciting life on distant shores.

* * *

My layover at Heathrow was long enough that I was able to wander the length of the departure terminal poking in and out of gift shops and bookstores without any real urgency. I eventually arrived at the gate and found a seat to camp until they called for boarding. About five minutes later the middle-aged couple from the bathroom arrived.

The announcement to board was incidental. The crowd in the terminal, eager to go, had begun to rise and organize as they knew the time had come. Boarding became an indiscriminant and anxious process.

So of course, we were delayed.

It began with an explanation from the pilot that the plane had been left on the wrong side of the tarmac and had to wait for planes to land before it could cross the runways to the gate. Then we had to wait for the plane to be fueled. Then, we had to wait for them to complete the paperwork about the fueling. Then we had to wait for a new place in the line of planes queued up for departure. Then, while waiting on the runway, we blew a fuse. (This explained why my headphones stopped working.) We had to return to the gate.

Then we had to wait to see if the fuse could be replaced.

Then we had to wait on the paperwork about the fuse.

Then we had to wait to be fueled again because of the fuel we had burned on the runway.

Then we had to wait for the paperwork about *this* fueling.

Then we had to wait, again, for our turn on the runway.

All told, we waited 3 hours in various phases of pre-flight and post-paperwork before we were underway.

The rest of the flight was uneventful. I was getting a sore throat and divided my time between sleeping to avoid jetlag, drinking all the soda they would bring me, and taking trips to the restroom, which was thankfully unremarkable.

* * *

We landed in Phoenix about the time the flight I was supposed to make was landing in Tucson.

I had cell service for the first time in over a week. I made my way to customs as I checked my messages. Just as I was being told no one had called to let me know they were planning to pick me up, a guard ordered me to turn off my phone. I did not know if I was interfering with his sensitive navigation instruments, or if the rules of passport control did not allow you a lifeline to call and get help with the answers.

Flying solo, I managed my way and was passed on to baggage claim. A long hike to the end of the rows of luggage belts brought me to a customs official who let me know that even though my bags were checked through to Tucson, I had to claim them here and bring them through.

By the time I went back to the belts and returned with my things, two substantial lines had formed. I chose the bigger one with nearly all airline crew and military personnel and was rewarded with quick passage by virtue of the momentum they created as they were all waved through.

Past the glass doors and to the immediate left was what appeared to be a hotel front desk where were stationed a bored security guard and an important looking man in a tie. I was told to go here to arrange for an alternate connection and to check my bags through if a flight was available.

I was put on a nine-something flight and was issued a new ticket. My bags were tagged and taken from me and I was sent on my way. I tried to follow another flight crew, but was told they were going to a special area. My insistence that wherever they were going looked more fun than where I was going got me a smile from the stewardess as she closed the door to their private hallway.

I followed the public routes down moving walkways and up elevators along with a knot of people from my London flight who were trying to make connections also. I emerged from the elevator in America.

* * *

People streamed back and forth, and swirled around and welcomed each other home. The smell, the noise, everything, was familiar again. I made my way to security.

I showed the young lady at the podium my ticket and she told me I'd have to go to the baggage check-in counter for a boarding pass. She was pleasantly surprised that I was not angry, frustrated, or in any way blaming her for this information. I got directions, wished her a good day, ducked the ropes, and headed downstairs.

I returned shortly with my pass. While I was downstairs I was refused service at the First Class check-in and had to wait in line while a woman denied having any explosives, but then volunteered helpfully that she did have several books of matches and a couple of lighters. I wondered how my fork was doing.

A different woman at the same podium looked over my boarding card and considered my passport before sending me to the x-ray line at the far left of the security area. She did this with a tone of voice that indicated that I was going to a Special Line for Special People for a Special Reason and that I would be stripped naked if I didn't do exactly what I was told. I examined my boarding pass to try and figure out how it had betrayed me.

Change, wallet, keys, pens, monocular, comb, change, jacket, belt, boots, scarf, and bags went into their appropriate bins and trays and were rolled into the x-ray machine. I stepped through the metal detector, grabbed my pocket things and bins, and was given an orange laminated card to hold as I stood in a line of One at the next checkpoint. I was waved through and I stepped up to the chair and mat with the yellow footprints on it where I'd be gone over with the wand.

My pockets were emptied again and I went through the motions automatically; lift this leg, that leg, stand up, arms so… The guard told me he was going to pat me down. I refused unless he bought me a drink first. He actually laughed. Then patted me down.

Afterward, I asked an elderly security agent about this whole business. I explained that I had been "randomly chosen by the airline for special screening" about four or five times now in the past year. He cackled my boarding pass, then explained in kind.

There was nothing random about it. The software flags you first for overseas travel when you're entering or leaving the country. Then you can get flagged for one-way travel. The software doesn't like that. I would have to talk to my travel agent about the creative nature of the round trips I was booked on.

Finally, I could get flagged at the baggage counter for being a woman, or being disabled.

So there I had it. Flagged if I do, Flagged if I don't. Flagged coming and going.

* * *

I had enough time to buy a sausage and walk to the gate before pre-boarding. In the waiting area there was a spontaneous reunion between a girl heading to Tucson and a girl coming from Colorado. I gathered that they had gone to High School together in Phoenix. The Tucson bound traveler complained to her friend that her last boyfriend was only interested in sex and she wished she wasn't so easy. She spent the rest of her time waiting to board talking to all the young men suddenly seated around her.

On board, the flight crew announced that we would be flying with Captain John and First Officer Tommy. Dear God, I was back in the States. I missed my fork, but at that moment I missed Captain Rodriguez more.

* * *

I arrived in Tucson late. No one had returned my phone calls. I was on my own getting back to the house. I gathered my bags, except for one I couldn't find. I finally went to customer service for the airline, where I was told the bag I had checked in back in Phoenix caught an earlier flight and was waiting for me behind the customer service counter.

I left Sunday morning and arrived Sunday night. The trip back took nearly twenty-four hours. I caught the shuttle bus and went home.

ABOUT THE AUTHOR

Robert J. Schulenburg is a native of San Jose, California. His career in Special Education has led him to serve in Central America and the Caribbean with the US Peace Corps. His study of culture, myth, and religion from around the world has heavily influenced his writing, prompting studies in how the condition of the individual influences and is influenced by the strange world we all live in.

You may send any correspondence for Robert to:

authors@samestrangeworld.com

www.ingramcontent.com/pod-product-compliance
Lightning Source LLC
Chambersburg PA
CBHW060711030426
42337CB00017B/2833